Child of the Moon

JEANNE COTTER

ILLUSTRATED BY CHRYSA OTTO

A MYTHIC RAIN BOOK

A *Mythic Rain* book
Published by Mythic Rain, Inc.
P.O. Box 11840
St. Paul, MN 55111
(888) 698-7362 (toll-free)
www.mythicrain.com

Library of Congress Cataloging-in-Publication Data available
ISBN 0-9672982-2-9 (reinforced for library use)
Printed in the United States of America
Printed on acid-free paper

10 9 8 7 6 5 4 3 2 1

*I would like to express my deepest appreciation to
Jaena JoWisniewski for her invaluable creative support.
– Jeanne Cotter*

BOOK ACKNOWLEDGEMENTS
Editor: Daniel Kantor, The Kantor Group, Inc., Minneapolis, MN
Copy editing: Kathleen Felong
Childhood psychological development consultation: Greg Knotts
Art direction and design: Jennifer Spong, The Kantor Group, Inc.
Production supervision: Matthew Moore, Mythic Rain, Inc., St. Paul, MN
Printing and binding: Worzalla, Stevens Point, WI
Prepress: Maximum Graphics, Chaska, MN
Author photograph: Mark Luinenburg

Watercolor illustrations painted on Arches 140# rough press watercolor paper
Display type set in Sabon, text type set in Sabon and Frutiger

CHILD OF THE MOON CD ACKNOWLEDGEMENTS
Music and lyrics: Jeanne Cotter
Lead vocal performance: Jeanne Cotter
Production and orchestral arrangement: Jeanne Cotter and Stephan Oberhoff
Engineering: Stephan Oberhoff, Full Circle Productions, Woodland Hills, CA
Flute, bamboo flute, alto flute and tenor flute: Pedro Eustache
Acoustic and electric piano: Jeanne Cotter
Violin: Richard Greene and Margaret Wooten
Acoustic and electric guitar: James Harrah
Keyboards: Stephan Oberhoff
Background vocals: Matthew Moore, Greg Knotts, Stephan Oberhoff

This book is dedicated to my precious

Godchild, Ruth Joana Manthey

My father taught me that "life is never separate from the land." This profound message continues to shape me, reminding me to honor the wisdom of creation. It is from my father that I also learned the power of storytelling, the oral tradition of passing on values from one generation to the next. *Child of the Moon* creates opportunities for essential storytelling between adult and child. It has been written to help pass on to our children the sacredness of life and our intimate connection with the earth, the sky and the circle of life where all are blessed.

Child of the Moon also introduces children to the language of symbolism by revealing strengths and key behaviors of the nature characters that befriend the reader throughout the book. To help illuminate the full potential of this book, I've included a "Glossary of Animal Symbols" for the young reader. In my "Notes from the Author" the deeper meaning of the text is explored and assistance is provided in storytelling and the use of symbols.

This story is unique in that it never really ends. Like nature, it is cyclical, encouraging rereading and reinterpretation. I invite you and the children you love to embark on this journey of self-discovery, sharing what is most meaningful in the ever-evolving stories of your lives.

Jeanne Cotter

When all the world is sound asleep,
the moon begins to rise.

He watches over your night dreams
and lights the blackened skies.

He rocks the ocean back and forth
like Grandma's wooden chair
and tumbles you into sleep's embrace
while I hold you near.

We'll carry the moon across the skies
and put it to sleep in your sweet eyes.
Then darkness and dreams won't frighten you,
my child of the moon…

my Child of the Moon.

Creation sings for the rising sun
as she climbs the sky into day —

a ball of fire and warmth and fun
to umbrella your summer play.

Each year her seasons will teach you more
of the mystery she knows.

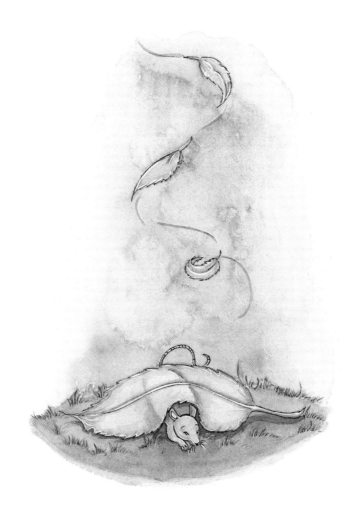

When the light and warmth seem lost,
        she's dancing in the shadows.

On the days she hides
        in the clouds above,
        just look in the faces of those you love.
It's there you'll find the shining sun,
            my child, darling one...

                    my Child of the Sun.

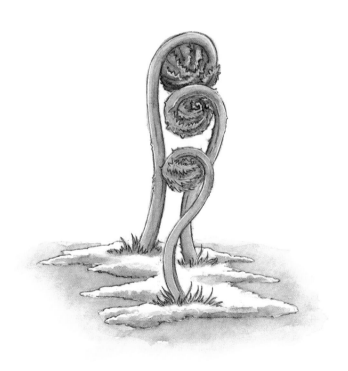

In the soft black earth
        each seed is blessed
and told the story of life,
        the secret of the redwood forest,
    the wonder of you tonight.

Each of us is given a garden
      to plant and water and weed.

Your song and your smile,
   your magic and dreams,
are the sun and
      the growing seed.

You are my garden, my joy and delight!
I give you the sun and the moon tonight,

but it's Mother Earth who
knows your song.
I'll be here to sing along…

my Child of the Earth.

My child...

my precious one.

Glossary of Animal Symbols How many places in this book can you find these animal friends?

Bats fly at night using sound waves to "see" with their ears rather than their eyes.

Deer sprint at great speeds, leaping and jumping gracefully as they go.

Eagles fly higher than any other bird and can see eight times farther than humans.

Bees can carry 300 times their own weight.

Dragonflies reflect and scatter the light of the sun in order to shine with bright rainbow colors.

Fish lay many eggs, giving life to new fish. They swim in groups called schools.

Butterflies can taste the sweetness of the flowers through their front feet.

Ducks use their own body oil to waterproof their feathers. This keeps them dry when in the water.

Foxes are good at blending into their environment. In the winter, some even turn white to match the snow.

CHILD OF THE SUN

The sun has long been honored, even worshiped by some cultures, as the symbol for energy, the life force of creation. The sun is the most brilliant of celestial bodies and is depicted in iconography as the very heart of the cosmos. As a source of heat, the sun represents vitality and fertility, but also the potential for devastation and drought. A contradictory symbol, the sun embodies the destructive and the regenerative forces of creation energy.

Creation energy is the transforming energy of change. To be a child of the sun, one must understand that change is a natural part of life. The life force and change go hand in hand. This process of conversion teaches us that life's dyings and disappointments can be opportunities for rebirth.

With the sun, come shadows. Unfortunately, our shadow side is often associated with the negative, even dangerous, part of our humanity. But the shadow as symbol is merely what we keep hidden, the side of the psyche that holds our biases, doubts and fears. It is also in the shadow that potential lies dormant. The shadow side is not to be ignored. Acknowledging our dark side can lead us into the light of understanding. To dance in the shadows is to address our own weaknesses and allow the birthing of our full potential.

Considered by early cultures to be the heart of the universe, the sun is symbolically linked to the human heart, the place believed to be the center of the body and the source of love. The fullness of life is not experienced without the immense gift of love. To be a child of the sun is to hold love as the highest value, for it is the wellspring from which the life force flows. It is the light in which one learns to plant, nurture and harvest one's own garden of potential. A child comes to know the value of love through the experience of being loved.

Butterfly

Most cultures symbolically link butterflies to transformation and the energy of creation. From caterpillar to chrysalis to flying insect, butterflies are a model of metamorphosis. In their evolved form, they dance on the flowers, able to taste the sweet nectar through receptors in their front feet. Butterflies remind us that through transformation we can experience the sweetness of life.

Eagle

American Indians believe that eagles are messengers from above, embodying the spirit of the sun and connecting heaven and earth. Baby eagles learn to fly by riding on their parents' backs. The young birds are then dropped and, in mid air, safely caught again. This cycle is repeated until the baby eagles can fly on their own. Eagles teach us to soar and reach for new heights.

Dragonfly

Dragonflies are powerful animal symbols connected to the sun. They have learned the magic of dancing with the light. Like a rainbow, structures in dragonflies' bodies refract light, giving them their iridescence. Dragonflies remind us to dance with our own light, allowing our beauty to shine.

Turtle

American Indians see turtles as reminders that Mother Earth provides for all of our needs. Hatching from eggs buried in the sand, the young turtles are left to fend for themselves. Mother Earth is their sole caregiver as they make their way to the waters. We learn from turtles that all we need is available to us. We are reminded to care for Mother Earth as she cares for us.

Spider

The spider is a feminine symbol associated with the weaving of human destiny. Spiders remind us that we are the authors of our own story, spinning it like a web with our emotions, thoughts and behaviors. Destiny — the unfolding of our story — always involves choice. It is by choice that we invest in our truest self or remain unfulfilled.

Frog

American Indians believe that the croaking of frogs could summon the "Thunder Beings" to send down the rains to cleanse and renew the land. Frogs are night singers, teaching us to sing our own stories in order to bring healing and renewal to ourselves, as well as to those around us.

Bee

Bees are able to carry 300 times their own weight, defying laws of aerodynamics in their flight. Bees symbolize the strength of the human spirit to carry a heavy burden and still flourish.

CHILD OF THE EARTH

A child of the earth understands that all of creation is blessed. It is Mother Earth who holds all things in a sacred circle of life. Personified in mythology as Gaia, Mother Goddess, the earth is traditionally viewed as the womb of life. It is from the earth that all life is born and to the earth that all life returns. Like the caterpillar going through the stages of metamorphosis to become a butterfly, so all of life is caught up in a constant and miraculous course of transformation.

In this story of life, the earth is a symbol of fertility and sustenance. The fecundity of the earth teaches children to accept the responsibility of making bountiful gardens of their own lives. Each child represents a fertile field, ripe with promise. A child of the earth is one who honors his or her instincts and natural talents, transforming potential into ability, weakness into opportunity, and dreams into reality.

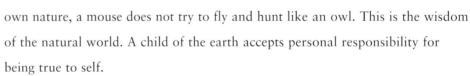

Earth is the element most associated with the gift of self-understanding. True to its own nature, a mouse does not try to fly and hunt like an owl. This is the wisdom of the natural world. A child of the earth accepts personal responsibility for being true to self.

Child of the Moon teaches children and adults that no one can fulfill the purpose of another. Each life has a specific calling, a unique reason it was dreamed into being.

We are companions for one another and for our children on this journey of life. We can best offer the wisdom of creation by our living example, embodying the symbolic gifts of the moon, the sun and the earth. As we share these gifts with our children, we do so freely, for they must create their own paths of understanding and self-expression. May we listen well as they sing their unique songs. — J.C.